DIGITAL CLASSROOMS

Unlocking Retirement Riches as an Online Tutor

ROBERT J BANNON

My mother used to say, "If you don't have something nice to say, don't say anything at all."

I've adapted it.

When you express negative opinions, the Universe will give you more negativity.

Instead, express gratitude and it will you give you more to be grateful for.

Thanks Mom

Contents

INTRODUCTION   VII

FORWARD   IX

1. ONLINE TUTORING   1

2. TUTORING PLATFORMS   5

3. WHAT TO TEACH   11

4. HOW MUCH   15

5. IMPORTANT TOOLS   19

6. CREATE A PROFILE   25

7. TUTORING VS. COACHING   31

8. BEING A PROFESSIONAL   37

9. TUTOR BENEFITS   43

10. LANGUAGE LEARNING SERVICE   47

11. BONUS MATERIAL   55

Afterword   60

About the Author   65

INTRODUCTION

Hey Super Savvy Seniors!

So, you've gracefully mastered the art of retirement, and now you're thinking, "What's next? World peace, perhaps?" Well, how about something a tad more achievable (and equally rewarding), as we step into the vibrant realm of online tutoring!

Picture this: You, with a cup of your favorite beverage, sharing your wisdom with eager learners from the comfort of your favorite armchair. Forget the chalk dust on your sleeves – it's time for virtual whiteboards and digital high-fives!

Embark on the Adventure of Knowledge: Say goodbye to the classroom drama and hello to the pixels of education! Online tutoring is your ticket to connect with curious minds from around the world. Whether you're a math maestro, a literary luminary, or a coding connoisseur, there's a virtual classroom waiting for your unique expertise.

Why Be a Sage on the Stage When You Can Be a Guide on the Glide: Wave farewell to the monotony of retirement and glide into the world of tutoring. Share your stories, sprinkle a little humor, and make learning an experience that's as delightful as your favorite sitcom rerun.

Flexibility that Beats Your Favorite Yoga Pose: No need to set the alarm for the crack of dawn! Choose your hours, create your schedule, and make room for that mid-morning nap. Online tutoring lets you be the captain of your own time ship.

No Need for the Commute – We're Keeping It Zen: Forget rush-hour traffic and say hello to your cozy sanctuary. With online tutoring, your living room transforms into the ultimate wisdom haven. Slippers, coffee, and imparting knowledge – what more could you ask for?

So, dear retirees, fasten your seatbelts (metaphorically speaking, of course), because the online tutoring adventure awaits! Your next chapter of imparting knowledge, making a difference, and maybe a few laughs along the way, starts here.

Cheers to the new-age sages, the digital mentors, and the retired rock stars of online tutoring!

FORWARD

Welcome to "***Digital Classrooms***: *Unlocking Retirement Riches as an Online Tutor*" – your comprehensive guide to navigating the virtual landscape and turning your passion for teaching into a rewarding retirement income. In the dynamic world of online education, the opportunities to shape minds and bolster your financial future have never been more promising.

As we embark on this enlightening journey, this book will serve as your compass, guiding you through the intricacies of online tutoring. Whether you're an experienced educator or a newcomer to the virtual classroom, our mission is to empower you with the knowledge and strategies needed to flourish in the digital teaching realm.

Explore the limitless potential of online tutoring and discover how your expertise can translate into a stream of income that fuels your retirement dreams. From optimizing your online presence to mastering effective teaching techniques, we'll cover it all. You can be sure that your virtual classroom stands out in the competitive online education landscape.

"Digital Classrooms" isn't just a book; it's your roadmap to unlocking the door to a retirement filled with both purpose and prosperity. Let's dive into the digital world, where every click brings you closer to the retirement riches you deserve.

Chapter 1

ONLINE TUTORING

O nline tutoring is a form of education where a tutor provides help or instruction to students over the internet. This method of tutoring has become increasingly popular because of advances in technology and the widespread availability of high-speed internet.

Here's an overview of how online tutoring works:

- **Platform Selection:** Online tutoring can take place on various platforms, ranging from dedicated tutoring websites to general education platforms. Some platforms connect tutors directly with students, while others act as intermediaries.

- **Communication Tools:** Tutors and students communicate through video calls, audio calls, chat, or a combination of these. Video conferencing tools, messaging apps, and virtual classrooms are very common methods for these interactions.

- **Subject Coverage:** Online tutoring covers a wide range of subjects, from academic subjects like math, science, and languages to specialized skills, such as music, coding, or test preparation. Tutors can cater to students of different ages and academic levels.

- **Scheduling and Flexibility:** One advantage of online tutoring is the flexibility it offers. Tutors and students can schedule sessions at mutually convenient times, and learners can access resources and support from the comfort of their homes.

- **Payment and Compensation:** Tutors can charge fees for their services, and the payment structure varies. Some tutors charge hourly rates, while others may have packages or subscription models. Payment is often facilitated through the tutoring platform or through other online payment methods.

- **Qualifications and Expertise:** Tutors typically have expertise in the subjects they teach. Some may be certified teachers, while others may have practical experience in a specific field. The qualifications and requirements can vary depending on the platform and the preferences of the students.

For retirees, online tutoring can be an excellent income idea, leveraging their years of experience and expertise. It allows them to share their knowledge with others while working from the comfort of their homes. It provides a flexible schedule, enabling retirees to balance work with other activities in their lives.

Chapter 2

TUTORING PLATFORMS

There are several popular online tutoring platforms that connect tutors with students. Each platform has its own features, requirements, and payment structures. Here are some of the main tutoring platforms and an overview of how they work:

1. **Wyzant:**

   - **How It Works:** Tutors create profiles detailing their expertise and experience. Students can search for tutors based on subject and location. The platform facilitates communication and scheduling, and sessions can be conducted online or in person.

○ **Payment:** Tutors set their own hourly rates, and Wyzant takes a percentage of the earnings.

2. **Chegg Tutors:**

○ **How It Works:** Tutors apply to become part of the platform and go through a vetting process. Students can connect with tutors for instant help or schedule sessions. The platform provides an online whiteboard for collaborative work.

○ **Payment:** Tutors are paid per minute for their time, and payments are made weekly.

3. **Tutor.com:**

○ **How It Works:** Tutors can apply to become part of Tutor.com's network. Students can connect with tutors for on-demand help or schedule sessions. The platform covers a wide range of subjects and provides tools for collaborative learning.

○ **Payment:** Tutors are paid hourly, and the exact rate depends on the subject.

4. **VIPKid:**

- **How It Works:** VIPKid connects English-speaking tutors with Chinese students for one-on-one online English lessons. The focus is on teaching English as a second language to children.

- **Payment:** Tutors are paid per lesson, and the rates are predetermined. The platform provides a flexible schedule.

5. **Skooli:**

- **How It Works:** Tutors create profiles, and students can search for and connect with tutors based on their expertise. The platform offers real-time, online tutoring with interactive tools.

- **Payment:** Tutors set their own rates, and Skooli takes a percentage of the earnings.

6. **Preply:**

- **How It Works:** Tutors create profiles, and students can search for tutors based on language, subject, and availability. The platform facilitates online lessons and provides tools for scheduling and communication.

- **Payment:** Tutors set their own hourly rates, and Preply takes a commission.

7. **LearnMate:**

- **How It Works:** LearnMate connects Australian students with tutors for in-person or online lessons. Tutors create profiles with their qualifications, and students can search for tutors based on subject and location.

- **Payment:** Tutors set their own rates, and LearnMate takes a percentage.

These platforms and others provide opportunities for both retired individuals and other professionals to offer their expertise in various subjects. It's essential for tutors to carefully read the terms, conditions, and payment structures of each platform before deciding to join. Building a strong and attractive profile can enhance a tutor's chances of being selected by students.

Chapter 3

WHAT TO TEACH

Online tutoring covers a wide range of subjects, catering to the diverse needs and interests of students. Some of the principal subjects covered include:

- **Mathematics:** Basic arithmetic, algebra, geometry, calculus, statistics, etc.

- **Science:** Physics, chemistry, biology, environmental science, etc.

- **Languages:** English, Spanish, French, Mandarin, etc.

- **Social Studies/History:** World history, U.S. history, geography, political science, etc.

- **Computer Science/Programming:** Coding languages, software development, computer applications, etc.

- **Test Preparation:** SAT, ACT, GRE, GMAT, language proficiency exams, etc.

- **Music and Arts:** Music theory, instrument lessons, drawing, painting, etc.

- **Business and Finance:** Accounting, economics, finance, entrepreneurship, etc.

- **Health and Wellness:** Nutrition, fitness, psychology, etc.

- **Foreign Languages:** Learning and practicing languages such as Spanish, French, German, etc.

For retiree tutors, there are niche areas that may be of interest, leveraging their years of experience and expertise. Here are some potential niche areas:

1. **Life Skills Coaching:** Sharing practical life skills, such as time management, goal setting, and communication, can be valuable for students preparing for adulthood.

2. **Career Guidance:** Retirees often have rich

professional experience. Providing guidance on career choices, resume building, and interview skills can be beneficial.

3. **Hobbies and Leisure Activities:** Tutors can share their passion for hobbies like gardening, photography, cooking, or any other leisure activity.

4. **Memoir Writing:** Helping students develop their writing skills by guiding them in creating personal memoirs or autobiographies. This will be of particular interest to other seniors.

5. **Mindfulness and Meditation:** Teaching relaxation techniques, mindfulness, and meditation for stress reduction and overall well-being.

6. **Local History and Culture:** Sharing insights into local history, traditions, and culture can be interesting, especially for students looking to learn more about their community.

7. **Interpersonal Communication:** Providing guidance on effective communication, active

listening, and conflict resolution.

8. **Creative Writing and Poetry:** Encouraging creativity through writing short stories, poems, or even helping with creative writing projects.

When considering a niche, it's essential to assess personal interests, skills, and the potential demand for the chosen subject. Tailoring tutoring services to unique niche areas can make retirees stand out and attract students who have specific learning goals in those areas.

Chapter 4

HOW MUCH

Tutoring rates can vary widely depending on factors such as the tutor's experience, the subject matter, the level of expertise required, and regional differences. The platform used for tutoring can influence rates and whether we do the tutoring online or in person. Here are some general examples of recent tutoring rates in the United States.

- **High School Subjects (e.g., Math, Science, English):**

  - Entry-Level Tutor: $20 - $40 per hour

  - Experienced Tutor: $40 - $75 per hour

  - Specialized or Advanced Subjects: $50 - $100+ per hour

- **Test Preparation (e.g., SAT, ACT, GRE):**

- $40 - $75 per hour for general test preparation

- $50 - $100+ per hour for specialized or advanced test preparation

- **College-Level Subjects:**

  - $50 - $100+ per hour, depending on the complexity of the subject

- **Language Tutoring:**

  - $20 - $50 per hour for common languages

  - $30 - $75+ per hour for less common or specialized languages

- **Music and Arts:**

  - $30 - $60 per hour for music lessons

  - $25 - $50 per hour for visual arts lessons

- **Specialized Skills (e.g., Coding, Computer Science).**

  - $40 - $80+ per hour

It's important to note that these are general ranges, and rates can vary. Tutors may charge more for specialized expertise, advanced education, or extensive experience. Some platforms may have their own pricing structures or simply take a percentage of the tutor's earnings.

Tutors, including retirees, should consider their own qualifications, the demand for their expertise, and the local market when setting their rates. It's also beneficial to research the rates charged by other tutors in the same subject and geographical area to remain competitive. As the tutoring landscape grows, these rates may change, so it's advisable to check current trends and averages in the relevant field.

Chapter 5

IMPORTANT TOOLS

Online tutors can enhance their teaching and support their students by providing various tools and resources. Here are some commonly used tools and resources for online tutoring, along with suggestions on where tutors can find them:

1. **Digital Whiteboard Platforms:**

    - **Tools:** Online whiteboards facilitate real-time collaboration. Tutors and students can draw, write, and share ideas.

    - **Resources:** Platforms like Explain Everything, BitPaper, and AWW App offer digital whiteboard functionalities.

2. **Video Conferencing Software:**

    - **Tools:** Video conferencing tools enable

face-to-face interaction and screen sharing.

- ○ **Resources:** Zoom, Skype, Microsoft Teams, and Google Meet are popular choices for online tutoring sessions.

3. Document Sharing and Editing:

- ○ **Tools:** Tutors can share documents for collaborative editing or review.

- ○ **Resources:** Google Docs, Microsoft OneDrive, and Dropbox allow easy sharing and editing of documents.

4. Interactive Quizzes and Polls:

- ○ **Tools:** Create quizzes and polls to assess understanding.

- ○ **Resources:** Kahoot!, Quizizz, and Poll Everywhere are interactive platforms for creating assessments.

5. Screen Recording Software:

- ○ **Tools:** Record tutorials or explanations for

later review and use.

- **Resources:** Loom, Screencast-O-Matic, and Camtasia allow tutors to create and share screen recordings.

6. Learning Management Systems (LMS):

- **Tools:** LMS platforms help organize and track student progress.

- **Resources:** Moodle, Canvas, and Google Classroom are LMS options for managing coursework and resources.

7. Interactive Educational Websites:

- **Tools:** Use interactive websites for engaging lessons.

- **Resources:** Khan Academy, BBC Bitesize, and interactive simulations on PhET Interactive Simulations can complement lessons.

8. Digital Flashcards:

- **Tools:** Create digital flashcards for review

and reinforcement.

- ◦ **Resources:** Quizlet and Anki are popular platforms for creating and sharing flashcards.

9. **E-books and Online Texts:**

- ◦ **Tools:** Share e-books and online texts for additional reading.

- ◦ **Resources:** Project Gutenberg, OpenStax, and Google Books offer a wealth of free and accessible texts. Consider creating your own books.

10. **Language Learning Apps:**

- ◦ **Tools:** Supplement language lessons with interactive language learning apps.

- ◦ **Resources:** Duolingo, Babbel, and Memrise are popular language learning apps.

11. **Subject-Specific Apps.**

- ◦ **Tools:** Use apps tailored to specific subjects.

○ **Resources:** For example, Desmos for math, ChemCollective for chemistry simulations, or GeoGebra for interactive geometry.

Tutors can find these tools and resources through online platforms, app stores, and educational websites. It's essential for tutors to explore and familiarize themselves with the tools that best suit their teaching style and the needs of their students. Many of these tools offer free versions or trials, making them accessible for tutors who may work independently or through tutoring platforms.

Chapter 6

CREATE A PROFILE

For retirees looking to offer online tutoring services, effectively displaying, confirming, and presenting their qualifications is crucial for building credibility and attracting potential learners. Here are some tips on how retirees can achieve this:

1. **Create a Professional Profile:**

   - Develop a comprehensive and professional online profile on tutoring platforms or your personal website.

   - Include a well-written bio that highlights your expertise, experience, and passion for teaching.

2. **Highlight Relevant Experience:**

   - Emphasize your relevant professional and

educational background. If you have a degree or certifications, mention them prominently.

○ Showcase any teaching or mentoring experience you have, whether it's formal or informal, along with any updated certifications.

3. **Detail Specialized Skills:**

○ Clearly outline the subjects or skills in which you have expertise. Specify any niche areas or specialized knowledge you can offer.

○ Mention any specific achievements or projects related to your tutoring focus.

4. **Incorporate Testimonials and Reviews:**

○ If possible, include testimonials or reviews from previous students or colleagues. Positive feedback can enhance your credibility.

○ Encourage satisfied learners to leave reviews on your tutoring profile or website.

5. **Use a Professional Photo:**

- Include a clear and professional profile picture. A friendly and approachable image can help build a connection with potential learners.

6. **Provide a Detailed Resume or CV:**

- Attach a resume or curriculum vitae (CV) that provides an in-depth overview of your professional background, education, and any relevant accomplishments.

- Ensure that your resume reflects your commitment to continuous learning and improvement.

7. **Offer a Free Introduction or Trial Session:**

- Provide potential learners with a free introduction or trial session. This allows them to experience your teaching style and assess your qualifications firsthand.

8. **Showcase Teaching Materials:**

- If you have created educational materials, lesson plans, or other resources, consider sharing samples to showcase your teaching approach and the quality of your content.

9. **Maintain a Professional Online Presence:**

- Make sure your online presence is consistent across platforms. Use the same professional photo, bio, and details on various websites or social media profiles.

- Keep your profiles up to date with any new qualifications or achievements.

10. **Stay Engaged in Professional Development.**

- Demonstrate your commitment to ongoing learning by participating in relevant workshops, courses, or certifications.

- Mention any recent professional development activities on your profile.

By effectively presenting qualifications, retirees can position themselves as knowledgeable and reliable tutors. Building a strong online presence, showcasing relevant experience, and providing evidence of successful teaching can instill confidence in potential learners and contribute to a successful tutoring venture.

Chapter 7

TUTORING VS. COACHING

While online tutoring and life coaching share some similarities, they primarily differ in their objectives, focus, and methodologies. Here are six key distinctions between online tutoring, life coaching, and other forms of adult-to-adult learning:

1. **Aim and Focus:**

   ○ **Online Tutoring:** Primarily focused on academic or skill-based learning. Tutors provide instruction, guidance, and support to help students understand and master specific subjects or skills.

   ○ **Life Coaching:** Geared toward personal development and goal achievement. Coaches work with clients to identify and overcome obstacles, set and achieve goals, and enhance overall well-being.

2. **Content and Expertise:**

- **Online Tutoring:** Typically involves the transfer of knowledge in specific subjects, academic areas, or skills. Tutors often have expertise in a particular field or subject matter.

- **Life Coaching:** Addresses a broader range of personal and professional development topics. Coaches may not provide sub-ject-specific content, but focus on em-powering individuals to make positive life changes.

3. **Learning Approach:**

- **Online Tutoring:** Emphasizes structured learning, often following a curriculum or academic program. The goal is to enhance knowledge and skills through instruction and practice.

- **Life Coaching:** uses a client-centred approach, where the coach helps individuals explore their own values, priorities, and aspirations. The emphasis is on self-discovery and personal growth.

4. **Client Relationship:**

- **Online Tutoring:** Typically involves a more structured and formal relationship, with a focus on achieving specific learning outcomes. The dynamic is usually more instructional.

- **Life Coaching:** Involves a collaborative and supportive relationship. Coaches work with clients to explore goals, identify obstacles, and develop strategies for personal and professional development.

5. **Outcomes:**

- **Online Tutoring:** Aims to improve academic performance, enhance skills, and achieve specific learning objectives. The focus is on measurable outcomes related to the subject matter.

- **Life Coaching:** Focuses on personal growth, self-discovery, and achieving individual goals. Outcomes may be less tangible and more subjective, such as increased self-confidence or improved work-life balance.

6. **Applicability:**

- **Online Tutoring:** Primarily applied in educational contexts, helping students at various levels, from K-12 to higher education, as well as adult learners seeking to gain specific skills.

- **Life Coaching:** Applicable in various life domains, including career development, personal relationships, health and wellness, and overall life satisfaction.

While online tutoring and life coaching serve distinct purposes, there can be overlap in certain scenarios. For example, adult learners seeking career development might benefit from both academic tutoring and life coaching to address skill gaps and enhance overall professional growth. Ultimately, the choice between online tutoring and life coaching depends on the individual's goals and the specific areas they want to address in their personal and professional lives.

Chapter 8

BEING A PROFESSIONAL

H ere are some additional considerations and information that potential online tutors should know before engaging in online tutoring:

1. **Legal and Ethical Guidelines:**

   ○ Familiarize yourself with any legal and ethical guidelines related to tutoring, especially when working with minors. Understand privacy laws, code of conduct, and any specific regulations that may apply in your region.

2. **Technology Requirements:**

   ○ Ensure that you have the technology and a stable internet connection. Familiarize yourself with the tools and platforms you'll be using for online tutoring sessions.

3. **Effective Communication Skills:**

- Strong communication skills are essential for online tutoring. Be clear and concise in your explanations and adapt your communication style to suit the needs of each student.

4. **Adaptability:**

- Be adaptable to different learning styles and levels. Tailor your tutoring approach to meet the unique needs and preferences of each student.

5. **Feedback and Improvement:**

- Be open to feedback from students and continuously seek ways to improve your tutoring methods. Creating a positive and constructive learning environment is the key to helping your students achieve success.

6. Time Management:

- Manage your time effectively to balance tutoring sessions, preparation, and any administrative tasks. Setting clear boundaries for your availability is important.

7. Building Rapport:

- Establish a positive and supportive relationship with your students. Building rapport and trust can enhance the learning experience and contribute to successful outcomes.

8. Marketing and Self-Promotion:

- If working independently, consider marketing yourself through social media, community bulletin boards, or online tutoring platforms. A well-crafted profile and positive reviews can attract more students.

9. Payment and Billing:

- Decide on your payment structure and clearly communicate it to students.

Whether you charge hourly rates, session packages, or have a subscription model, transparency is key.

10. **Record Keeping:**

- Keep organized records of your tutoring sessions, including topics covered, progress made, and any feedback received. This information can be valuable for future sessions and evaluations.

11. **Professional Development:**

- Stay engaged in continuous professional development. Attend webinars, workshops, or courses to enhance your teaching skills and stay informed about educational trends.

12. **Insurance Considerations:**

- Depending on your location and the nature of your tutoring, investigate whether or not you need professional liability insurance. This can provide coverage in case of any unforeseen issues.

13. **Safety and Security:**

- Prioritize safety and security, especially when working with minors. Ensure that online interactions are conducted in a secure and private environment and follow best practices for online safety.

14. **Understanding the Needs of Different Learners.**

- Recognize that students have diverse learning needs and backgrounds. Be inclusive and accommodating and adapt your teaching style to meet the unique requirements of each learner.

By considering these factors, retirees can set themselves up for a successful and rewarding experience in the world of online tutoring. It's important to continuously learn, adapt, and refine your approach based on the needs of your students and the evolving landscape of online education.

Chapter 9

TUTOR BENEFITS

Online tutoring can offer retirees a range of possibilities and benefits, making it a viable and fulfilling option for you:

- **Flexibility and Convenience:**

Retirees can enjoy flexible schedules, choosing when and how often they want to tutor. This flexibility allows for a good work-life balance.

- **Work from Home:**

Online tutoring enables retirees to work from the comfort of their homes, eliminating the need for commuting and providing a convenient and stress-free work environment.

- **Use Expertise and Experience:**

Retirees can leverage their years of professional experience and expertise to help students succeed academically or develop specific skills, contributing meaningfully to the learning process.

- **Extra Income:**

Online tutoring can serve as a source of supplemental income for retirees. They can set their own rates and choose the number of hours they want to dedicate to tutoring.

- **Mentorship and Impact:**

Retirees can serve as mentors and make a positive impact on the lives of students. Sharing knowledge and life experiences can be rewarding and fulfilling for the tutor and in some cases, life-changing for the student.

- **Stay Mentally Active:**

Engaging in online tutoring allows retirees to stay mentally active and continue using their cognitive skills. It provides a sense of purpose and ongoing intellectual stimulation.

- **Explore Niche Areas of Interest:**

A retiree can focus on niche areas of interest or expertise, tailoring their tutoring services to subjects or skills that align with their passions.

- **Adapt to New Technologies:**

Online tutoring provides an opportunity for retirees to adapt to and stay current with new technologies, enhancing their digital literacy and staying connected in a technologically advancing world.

- **Personal Fulfillment:**

Helping others succeed and achieve their educational or personal goals can bring a sense of personal fulfillment and satisfaction to retirees.

- **Community Engagement:**

Online tutoring can foster connections within the global community. Retirees may interact with students from various geographic locations and backgrounds, promoting cultural exchange and understanding.

- **Continuous Learning:**

Engaging in tutoring activities allows a retired person to continue learning and growing. They may come across new challenges and gain insights from their interactions with students.

- **Positive Social Interaction.**

Online tutoring provides an avenue for positive social interaction. Retirees can build relationships with students, fostering a sense of connection and camaraderie.

•

Chapter 10

LANGUAGE LEARNING SERVICE

If you are fortunate enough to speak multiple languages, this could be a terrific niche to enter. Research existing resources and look for areas that are not being serviced and that you could help people with. This is a unique and somewhat more complex area than we have been covering to date. It may, however, be perfect for you. Creating and selling language learning resources can be a rewarding venture, especially considering the increasing demand for effective language learning tools. Here is a random selection of language learning resources you could create and sell:

1. **Digital Language Courses:**

   ○ Develop comprehensive digital language

courses covering various proficiency levels. Include video lessons, interactive exercises, quizzes, and downloadable materials.

2. **Customizable Learning Plans:**

- Offer personalized learning plans tailored to individual needs. This could involve assessments to determine proficiency levels and the creation of customized study schedules.

3. **Audio Lessons and Podcasts:**

- Create audio lessons or podcasts that focus on language pronunciation, vocabulary, and everyday conversations. These resources can be very appealing for today's consumer on the go.

4. **Grammar Guides:**

- Develop detailed grammar guides with explanations, examples, and exercises. Provide practical tips for mastering grammar rules in a user-friendly format.

5. **Flashcards and Vocabulary Lists:**

- Create digital flashcards and vocabulary lists that cover essential words and phrases. Include audio pronunciations to aid in learning pronunciation.

6. **Cultural Immersion Resources:**

- Offer resources that provide insights into the culture associated with the language. This could include videos, articles, or interactive content that enhance cultural understanding.

7. **Interactive Apps:**

- Develop language learning apps with interactive features, game elements, and real-time feedback. These apps can make language learning engaging and accessible.

8. **Writing and Speaking Prompts:**

- Create writing and speaking prompts to help learners practice expressing themselves in the language. Include feedback or model responses for self-assessment.

9. Live Online Classes:

- Host live online classes or webinars where learners can interact with instructors in real-time. This allows for direct feedback and a more immersive learning experience.

10. Language Challenges and Quizzes:

- Design language challenges and quizzes to gamify the learning process. Offer rewards or certificates for completing challenges and achieving specific milestones.

11. Textbooks and E-books:

- Write comprehensive textbooks or e-books that cover language fundamentals, grammar rules, and practical language usage. Offer them in both digital and print formats.

12. Pronunciation Guides:

- Develop resources specifically focused on pronunciation, including guides, exercises, and practice materials. Audio components are crucial for mastering correct pronunciation.

13. **Exam Preparation Materials:**

- Create resources geared towards language proficiency exams. Include practice tests, study guides, and strategies for succeeding in language exams.

14. **Language Learning Journals:**

- Design printable or digital language learning journals that help learners track their progress, set goals, and reflect on their language learning journey.

15. **Cultural Conversation Simulations:**

- Develop interactive simulations or scenarios that simulate real-life conversations in cultural contexts. This helps learners practice language skills in practical situations. It will also help them find the bathroom faster.

16. Business Language Resources:

- Create language resources tailored for business communication. This could include vocabulary related to industry-specific terminology, business etiquette, and communication skills.

17. Children's Language Learning Materials:

- Design language learning resources specifically for children, such as interactive games, storybooks, and videos that make learning fun and engaging.

18. Virtual Reality Language Experiences:

- Explore the use of virtual reality to create immersive language learning experiences. This could involve virtual trips, interactive scenarios, and cultural exploration.

19. Collaborative Learning Platforms:

- Establish an online platform that facilitates collaborative learning. This could include discussion forums, group projects, and peer-to-peer language exchange features.

20. **Subscription-based Learning Models.**

○ Offer subscription-based models where learners pay a recurring fee for access to a variety of language learning resources, updates, and new materials.

Remember to market your language learning resources effectively through your website, social media, and partnerships with language schools or online learning platforms. Providing valuable and engaging content, coupled with effective marketing, can make your language learning resources stand out in a competitive market.

In summary, online tutoring, as a business opportunity for retirees, offers a flexible, fulfilling, and intellectually stimulating way to share your knowledge, make a positive impact, and earn supplemental income. The adaptability of online platforms makes it accessible to retirees, allowing them to create a meaningful and rewarding post-retirement career.

Chapter 11

BONUS MATERIAL

FINDING A NICHE

In this book and throughout this series, we often refer to finding a niche. We cannot overemphasize the importance of this. Identifying a niche market is a crucial step in developing a successful marketing strategy. Here are some effective ways to identify a niche:

1. **Understand Your Interests and Expertise.**

   ○ Consider your own interests, hobbies, and expertise. If you are passionate about a particular subject, you may have a better understanding of the needs and preferences of potential customers in that niche.

2. **Research Market Trends.**

- Stay updated on current market trends. Look for emerging industries or areas where there is a growing demand. Analyze market reports, industry publications, and news to identify potential niches.

3. **Identify Gaps in the Market.**

- Look for gaps or unmet needs in existing markets. Identify problems that are not adequately addressed and consider how your product or service could fill that void.

4. **Target Specific Demographics.**

- Consider targeting specific demographics such as age groups, professions, or geographic locations. Tailoring your products or services to a specific group can help you stand out in the market.

5. **Conduct Keyword Research.**

- Use tools like Google Keyword Planner, SEMrush, or Ahrefs to identify popular search terms related to your industry. This can give you insights into what people are actively searching for.

6. **Social Media Listening.**

- ○ Monitor social media platforms to understand conversations and trends within your industry. Social media listening tools, like Hootsuite and Google Alerts, can help you identify topics that are gaining traction.

7. **Customer Surveys and Feedback.**

- ○ Gather feedback from existing customers, or conduct surveys to understand their needs, preferences, and frustrations. This can provide valuable insights into potential niche opportunities.

8. **Competitor Analysis.**

- ○ Analyze your competitors to see where they are succeeding and where they may be falling short. Identifying areas where you can offer something unique or better can help you carve out a niche.

9. **Evaluate Your Unique Value Proposition (UVP).**

   ◦ Clearly define what sets your product or service apart from others. Your unique value proposition should address a specific need or problem in a way that is distinct from competitors.

10. **Check for Regulatory or Legal Restrictions.**

   ◦ Be aware of any legal or regulatory restrictions in potential niches. Some industries may have specific regulations that could affect your ability to enter or operate within a niche.

11. **Consider Long-Tail Keywords.**

   ◦ Long-tail keywords are more specific and can show niche areas within a broader market. Focus on these keywords to identify and target niche audiences. Generally, long tail keywords are phrases of 3 words or more.

12. **Check the negatives.**

- Negative reviews of other products or services in your niche are a great way to understand what potential customers are looking for. Fill the gap.

Remember, it's essential to thoroughly research and validate potential niches before committing resources. Testing and iterating based on feedback will help you refine your approach and better serve your niche audience.

Afterword

And there you have it, my delightful retirees, the curtain call to your grand entrance into the dazzling world of online tutoring!

As you embark on this new adventure, remember: You are not just sharing knowledge; you're crafting a symphony of wisdom, turning virtual pixels into moments of brilliance.

So, why should you dive into the world of online tutoring with the exuberance of a dancing diva? Here's why:

- **Endless Laughs:**

  - Who said learning can't be fun? Bring your humor, your stories, and your quirks to make every session fun and entertaining.

- **Flexitime Fiesta:**

  - Forget the 9-to-5 grind! Online tutoring lets

you be the captain of your own ship, navigating the waves of wisdom on your own time.

- **Techie Triumphs:**

  ◦ Embrace the tech magic! Conquer digital tools and whiteboards with the finesse of a magician, proving that you can teach an old dog new tricks.

- **Life-Long Learning:**

  ◦ You've retired from one chapter; why not start another? Become a forever learner and share the joy of continuous growth with your virtual pupils.

- **Mentorship Marvels.**

  ◦ Watch as you transform into a digital mentor, guiding your students not just academically, but through the maze of life.

Remember, you're not just a tutor; you're a beacon of inspiration, a fountain of knowledge, and a retiree who refuses to be bound by conventional timelines.

So, my retired friends, grab your digital capes, adjust your virtual spectacles, and get ready to soar into the hearts and minds of learners worldwide. The stage is set, the virtual applause awaits, and the world is ready for the retiree tutors to shine like the radiant stars you are!

Here's to the joy of teaching, the thrill of learning, and the endless possibilities that come with being an online tutor extraordinaire. Happy tutoring, and may your virtual classrooms be filled with laughter, wisdom, and boundless joy!

This series of books, **EXTRA RETIREMENT INCOME IS SEXY**, includes many, many possibilities for retirees to add more income and enjoy more creative pursuits. Here is a brief review of the other books:

Freelance Writing: Many websites and businesses constantly need content. If you enjoy writing, you could offer your services as a freelance writer. There are platforms like Upwork and Fiverr that connect writers with clients. We will explore this opportunity in depth in book 2, **THE PROSPEROUS PEN**.

Online Tutoring: If you have expertise in a particular subject, you could offer online tutoring services. Platforms like Chegg Tutors or Wyzant allow you to connect with students seeking help. More information about online tutoring is available in book 3 of this series, **DIGITAL CLASSROOMS**.

Virtual Assistance: Many entrepreneurs and small businesses need help with tasks like email management, data entry, and scheduling. Offering virtual assistance services can be a great way to use your organizational skills. We will dive into becoming a virtual assistant in book 4, **SILVER HAIRED SAGE**.

Sell Handmade Crafts or Digital Items: If you have a talent for crafting or have accumulated unique vintage items, you can sell them on platforms like Etsy or eBay. Creating digital products like ebooks, courses and journals can lead to a world of opportunity. This exciting area of income generation is fully explained in book 5, **DESIGNING WEALTH.**

Take part in Online Surveys and Reviews: While this may not generate a substantial income, participating in online surveys can provide a small stream of income. Websites like Swagbucks or Survey Junkie offer opportunities to earn money for your opinions. Creating and sharing product reviews can lead to a very substantial income generating business. We offer all the details of this business idea in book 6, ***GOLDEN INSIGHTS***.

About the Author

Robert J Bannon is still trying to define what retirement is and how to live it. Leveraging his life as an entrepreneur, sales manager, stockbroker and VP investor relations, along with 10 years as a tax consultant, Bob has written a 6 book series, EXTRA RETIREMENT INCOME IS SEXY, to help retirees create additional income and fulfillment in their life. He has also authored several other non-fiction titles, some of which are included below.

He and his wife live in the foothills of the Rockies and have 2 adult children and 3 grandsons. He continues to travel the world, play golf, and write, balanced with grocery shopping, cooking, and afternoon naps. You can reach him through his website at RobertJBannon.com.

Also By Robert J Bannon

EXTRA RETIREMENT INCOME IS SEXY
Ignite Your Financial Passion and Live the
Lifestyle You Love
BOOK 1
Paperback ISBN 978-0-9739646-9-1
Ebook ISBN 978-1-7382603-0-0

THE PROSPEROUS PEN
Mastering Freelance Writing for Retirement
Riches
Book 2
Paperback ISBN 978-1-7382603-1-7
Ebook ISBN 978-1-7382603-2-4

DIGITAL CLASSROOMS

Unlocking Retirement Riches as an Online Tutor

Book 3

Paperback ISBN 978-1-7382603-3-1

Ebook ISBN 978-1-7382603-4-8

SILVER HAIRED SAGE

Retirees Become Amazing Virtual Assistants & Increase Their Own Income

Book 4

Paperback ISBN 978-1-7382603-5-5

Ebook ISBN 978-1-7382603-6-2

DESIGNING WEALTH

A Retiree's Guide to More Income and Creative Fulfillment

Book 5

Paperback ISBN 978-1-7382603-7-9

Ebook ISBN 978-1-7382603-8-6

GOLDEN INSIGHTS

Unlocking Extra Income – A Retiree's Guide to Surveys & Reviews

Book 6

Paperback ISBN 978-1-7382603-9-3

Ebook ISBN   978-1-7382622-0-5

EASY STOCK MARKET STARTER COURSE
ASIN B09NCFC2FF   ISBN 979-8783059315

THE WEST COAST TRAIL: One Step at a Time
ASIN 172789703X   ISBN 978-1727897036

HOW TO WRITE A BOOK ABOUT WEIGHT LOSS
And any other non-fiction topic
ISBN PAPERBACK 978-1-7382622-1-2
ISBN E-BOOK   978-1-7382622-2-9

By Lonewolf Notes/RJB
ETSY SHOP MANAGER
ASIN B083XW6CXJ   ISBN 979-8601305228

MY WINE TASTING JOURNAL & NOTEBOOK
ASIN 1676781633   ISBN 978-1676781639

FINANCIAL PLANNER TEMPLATE
ASIN 1676048227   ISBN 978-1676048220

www.ingramcontent.com/pod-product-compliance
Lightning Source LLC
Chambersburg PA
CBHW070945210326
41520CB00021B/7058